MW01294354

THE SNOW HORSE

THE SNOW HORSE
A Round Up of Western Poetry

by Narrvel E. Hall

FOX HOLLOW
STORY PRESS
Malad City, Idaho
2014

Copyright © 2014 by Narrvel E. Hall

All rights reserved. This book or any portion thereof may not be reproduced or used in any manner whatsoever without the express written permission of the publisher except for the use of brief quotations in a book review or scholarly journal.

First Printing: 2014
ISBN 978-1-312-03168-5

Fox Hollow Story Press
125 North 5400 West
Malad City, ID 83252

Ordering Information:
Special discounts are available on quantity purchases by corporations, associations, educators, and others. For details, contact the publisher at the above listed address.

U.S. trade bookstores and wholesalers: Please contact Fox Hollow Story Press email naejhall@gmail.com.

Introduction and Dedication

This modest collection of poems had its beginnings over 30 years ago, when I discovered a need to somehow access my right brain to articulate and preserve, in an entertaining format, my own and other family stories.

Although I have cultivated a reputation for clear and cogent left-brain legal writing, polished by many years of law practice, I am the first to admit that my prose is technical and boring when applied to the larger world around me. I was inspired by the work of modern cowboy poets like Waddie Mitchell and Wallace McRae, who spoke the language of my youth, to try to write verse in the vernacular of the true West. This style seemed to fit my extended family and my experiences in the real world outside the law.

My shift to writing in verse was well received by the circles to whom it was recited, the Davis Arts Council in Layton, Utah, church social events in Utah and Idaho, open Mic sessions at the National Cowboy Poetry Gathering in Elko, Nevada, and the monthly meetings of the Ben Lomond Poets Association in Odgen, Utah. You, the reader, can judge for yourselves whether the detour into creativity has been worth the effort.

This collection is dedicated to my paternal grandparents, Leonard P. and Charlotte Hall, in whose home I spent many happy days and nights as a child and in whom I found a mix of grace and toughness instilled by pioneer upbringing and survival through three decades of the late 1800's and six decades in the 1900's. A portion of their life story is recited in my poem, "The Bull."

Acknowledgments

I would like to thank my talented daughter Melanie, whose expertise in assembling and publishing printed works, has finally put my scanty work product into book form. Thanks is also due to Vicki Moody, my longtime secretary/assistant, who patiently transcribed scribbled longhand compositions, with immeasurable cross-outs and interlineations, into intelligible English verse, and assembled the poems into a collection, with some logical (to the extent that logic can be said to apply to my handiwork) organization into chapters.

Thanks is also expressed to my lovely** wife Jeanmarie, who has patiently endured my idiosyncrasies for over 50 years of marriage and has, less patiently, but with unfailing grace tolerated my occasional clumsy attempts to make her the subject of my musing and scribbling.

Finally, thanks are due to numerous friends and relatives, whose stories or horse keeping properties have found their way into my poems. Some of these sources, who may or may not be, acknowledged in the text or footnotes of poems, are friends and neighbors Eulalie and Barry Howard, Pam and Jeff Gibson, Tim and Jan Edwards, and Peggy Morgan; and relatives, my wife's late parents, Myrtle and Ephraim Miller, my late parents, Pearl and Leonard Hall, and my late grandparents Charlotte and LP. Hall, the latter's hardscrabble accounts having started me on the quest to capture family "his-story" in verse.

**Editor's note: Jeanmarie Hall violently objected to the use of the term "lovely" and was emphatic that it be changed to "long-suffering" and "extraordinary" (or extraordinarily long-suffering), which Narrvel refused but agreed to include in this notation.

NARRVEL E. HALL grew up on farms and ranches in remote southern Idaho. He became involved with the Western Folk Life Center as a member of the Board of Trustees two decades or so ago through his love of cowboy poetry and all things western.

Narrvel is an attorney in Salt Lake City, Utah, where he has served as Chair of the Tax Section of the Utah State Bar, Chairman of the Salt Lake Estate Planning Council and as a member of the Board of Trustees of the Mountain States Pension Conference. He has served on the boards of Trustees of a number of charitable and cultural tax-exempt organizations and currently serves on the board of the Foundation for Hospice – Northern Utah, and the Oneida County, Idaho Planning and Zoning Commission.

Narrvel is active in his church and has served in numerous positions. He and his wife, Jeanmarie, have five children and 13 grandchildren. They live on a farm in Idaho where Narrvel looks forward to continuing his pastimes of raising and training horses, making saddles, painting, writing poetry and whatever else he has time to do between hay crops, as he phases into active partial retirement.

" *Now before the Bar I safely spare, I need no learned tome.*
Every day in my attaché I bring horse manure from home. "

From *Autobiography*

CONTENTS

I. FAMILY STORIES

AUTOBIOGRAPHY

It's not lack of strife in the country life,
or the space that heaven sent,
it's the quick availability
of tons of excrement;

If you come to harm down on the farm
or your health becomes unsure,
you soon forget both pain and grief,
knee-deep in wet manure;

When I was small and not too tall
and chewing gum was rare,
I lost, then found it seven times,
while feeding chickens there;

While milking cows and slopping sows
and waiting for love to bloom,
I was surely saved from grave mistake
by animal perfume;

Came college test in the B.S. quest,
slick Athena's mount got steeper
because the tenured Ph.D.s
just piled it higher and deeper;

Now before the bar, I safely spar,
I need no learned tome,
every day in my attaché
I bring horse manure from home.

Leonard Parley Hall
b. 4/8/1870 – d. 4/21/1961

Charlotte Morris Hall
b. 2/14/1871 – d. 5/7/1959

THE BULL

Grandpa knowed he was tough, his whole life had been rough,
he'd sheared sheep, busted sod and drove freightin,[1]
his knuckles was scarred an his body was hard,
an he'd lived through his fair share of hatin';

In much younger days he'd had vagabond way
an was knowed to have travelled by boxcars,
he'd drunk from a jug, an smoked an chewed plug,
an gone knuckle an skull in the bars;

Now they say that conversion can be quick as emersion,
but religion growed slower on him,
takin full forty years an a well fulla tears,
til his old mother's spirit was dim;

But, as she laid a dyin, he promised, not lyin,
to give up his hell bounden search,
an good as his word jug an pipe was interred,
an his wagon was soon saw at church;
Grandma Lottie knowed best, the pain of that quest,

she'd loved 'im fer most of her life,
thru good times an bad an the nine[2] kids she'd had,
in twenty odd years as his wife;

When he got that durned bull his conversion was full,
or so Grandpa 'lowed that was right,
but Grandma knowed well what he sometimes would tell,
that he still shorely loved a good fight;

Grandpa 'lowed he afeared neither man, haired ner sheared,
ner any durn four footed critter,
other church men[3] feared changes with drunk 'pokes at dances,
so he was the disgnate hitter;

On that Pioneer Day, in the usual way,
fer the local folks high entertainment,
they borrowed the bull so the buck chutes was full,
and the yard birds made shore his detainment;

---

1 Grain wagons to the rail head at Corrine, Utah
2 Two died in infancy
3 He served for years as counselor to the Bishop of the Malta, Idaho LDS Ward

Then the jingle-bobbed[4] punchers an bare-heeled lunchers,
an whomso had somethin to prove,
forked the broncs an the cattle an bravely done battle,
til they all was too stove up to move;

Grandpa's bull got some flustered, he bellered an blustered,
an pawed up c'ral dust a plenty,
but he never quite caught 'em, tho he plumb always fought 'em,
an he finished the day ought for twenty;

Then back to the farm, still threatenin harm,
that ton of baloney was put,
an soon face to face on his own ole' home place,
Grandpa carelessly braced 'im afoot;

He pawed gravel an rocks an rattled his hocks,
an struck a most arrogant pose,
spite of head shakin fuss and green splattered muss,
Grandpa grabbed fer the ring in his nose;

In the interest of beauty an all Christian duty,
he kened that bull needed religion,
so he walloped 'im good in the yard where he stood,
but that frightened the bull not a smidgeon;

Then the bull hit 'im dead in the chest with its head,
an knocked 'im down flat on his back
then butted an rolled 'im , an pinned 'im to home 'im ,
an pushed till he heard the bones crack;

But Grandpa held gamely, tho a little more lamely,
to the copper-clad, slime-covered ring,
the bull backed a little and bellerin spittle,
gave Grandpa an overhead swing;

Belly up on its shoulder he commenced to feel older,
fast losin his zeal to convert,
the bull took a notion in one down'ard motion,
slammed 'im face down in the dirt;

So the bull found 'is weakness an notin dazed meekness,
repeated the swingin routine,
as the ground rose to crash 'im an the bull tried to mash 'im ,
Grandpa judged 'at the bull had gone mean;

4 Spurs with metal clappers to make the rowels ring

When he hear'd his ribs break, he d'cerned his mistake,
an commenced to wish't he'd been more careful,
when his hip joints was jammed, an his backbone was slammed,
his spirit begun to be prayerful;

So he let out a yelp for someone to help,
he was lucky young Deward could hear 'im ,
tho he still held the ring in the bull's nose,
the thing, was he knowed he was started to fear 'im;

Then fin'ly his son fetched the ol' twelve gauge gun,
an demanded that bull's full attention,
in the side, point blank ranged, loads of buckshot soon changed
the bull's appetite fer contention;

The bull stumbled away, an soon died where he lay,
from a wound near the size of a plate,
as for Grandpa he groaned, and then later just moaned,
as they dragged 'im inside to his mate;

He'd been hurt before maybe ten times or more,
like the time when he chopped off his toe,[5]
but he'd never been shattered in places that mattered,
or where womenfolks' needles can't sew;

They fetched ol Doc Sater an soon or later
got some of the pieces to knit;
but the news was real bad an it troubled my dad
that he'd never again walk or sit;

But the churchmen made rounds an made ministrin sounds,
and the hipbones somehow found their places,
an with some better feelin, with back and legs healin,
Grandpa laughed at the docs to their faces;

So he slowly begun first to shuffle then run,
but he gave up bull fightin and brawlin,
an past seventy-five, Grandpa still much alive,
raced this nine year old grandson full haulin,[6]

After Lottie was gone Grandpa still carried on,
testified to the whole congregation
that repentance kin mend, so you see at the end,
both Grandpa an bull met salvation.

---

5 His mother-in-law sewed it back on and it survived, but protruded downward at a peculiar angle
6 Actually age 79, he beat me by twenty yards over a quarter mile after giving me a ten second head
start, and I thought I was pretty fast

CLEAR CREEK HOME FRONT

It's been said before about most any war,
so hell on the home front's no surprise,
but they don't tell the cost of home battles lost,
because armies take all the supplies;

During World War Two, most at home just made do,
the war machine was a great glutton,
Uncle Sam, to our grief, took all of the beef
so the home folks ate "government mutton;"[1]

While their uncles and sons fought the "Nips" and the "Huns"[2]
folks did without sugar and shoes,
ration books country wives took as facts of their lives,
but black market got all they could use;

Transportation was slow, when Dad's car wouldn't go,
when gas couldn't be bought any more;
so by two-horse-power wagon with old hay rack saggin
we made the six miles to the store;[3]

It was root hog or die and we barely got by,
so the shortages weren't really funny,
but to add to the harm, that rented dirt farm
grew varmints and bugs but no money;

Coyotes and big cats moving down to the flats
sometimes laid their tracks past our door,
though tracks didn't scare us,[4] the bugs didn't spare us,
it's mosquitoes that won in our war;

---

1 Venison
2 No ethnic disrespect intended. Those were the current slang terms for the enemy
3 Mary's Merc; Naf, Idaho
4 Except for Mom, who was even scared of big birds

They flew up in clouds and descended in crowds,
sucking man, bird and beast nearly dry,
Dad found no resource to fight that air force
that behaved like a Nazi ally;

The cows' milk was bloody and the horses were muddy,
their frantic behavior was scary,
so Mom was relieved when she finally received
her folks' offer of far sanctuary;

With the stock all stampeding and the family all bleeding,
Dad finally admitted defeat,
kids and Mom fled by car and behind us not far
Dad and cows made their wounded retreat.

THE MANTLE (OF EPHRAIM)

The man could not be born full grown
nor could the infant feel Godward gratitude,
yet mind and body know each lesson shown
as the Master Teacher teaches rectitude;

From royal Ephraim's clan, for him well named,
in golden curls and lacy collar posed,
the child before the man peers yet from photo framed,
in wonderment at later lessons closed;

Why, he seems to ask, could I not stay
while robust youth in simpler time and pace,
content to steward others' cows and hay,
nor ever back and back to learning's place?

The rustic cowboy grown, from pictured child,
scarce felt the unseen hand whose touch remained
to draw unerringly his feet, till reconciled,
to mission in dim eons past ordained;

From learning's halls at length a teacher rose
to shape two generations timely born,
with pupils, fellow teachers, and he chose
a path the Master Teacher could not mourn;

For in the very time this teacher came,
to place but little known, he thought to teach,
a larger mission then burst clear, not all the same,
a call received to grasp beyond his reach;

He had not thought to teach the common judge
nor yet preside, in stake with heads more hoar,
still, guided by the Master Teacher's nudge,
for decades he that mantle gravely wore;

Query now, what conscious choices torn
from plans, by keys and service in The Plan?
we see but darkly now of burdens borne
and how the priestly callings shaped the man;

But this is clear, that priesthood served, humanity improves,
and reach extends by standing on the Master Teacher's back;
and all are blessed by that humanity, that moves,
lifts, heals and teaches those who lack;

Now the Master Teacher watches where the pace of pain is slow,
a patriarch emeritus and the toddler on the wall
can only wait and hope at home as family come and go,
and Granddad Ephraim patiently awaits another call.

THE PROM

The fall of '57, in my senior year
at school,
opinions was divided, was I a honyock
or a fool;

I was boiled owl tough in football
stayin in the games both ways,
In the classroom riding easy,
tyin up them B's and A's;

I was bringin home the bacon, shot both
Bambi an his mother,
An Dad snubbed me on a buckskin colt,
we green broke for Mom's brother;

I could chew the rag with humans, gave
church speeches north an south,
But was tongue-tied by them fillies,
sufferin from a wooden mouth;

I just didn't speak the language
to say what was on my mind,
my social life was hoodooed,
I was flying dumb an blind;

I went stag to all the dances,
gave the belly rub a fling,
an I liked to sweat the wall flowers
with the jitterbug or swing;

I had seldom used a telephone
a major teenage sin,
though we had one for a year or two,
I wasn't buyin in;

I was mindin my digestion when my sister
tossed the bomb,
that her friend, the redhaired Jeanie,
must be taken to the prom;

She sez it was all decided,
Jean and friends made a decree,
that the needed decoration
for her formal gown was me;

Jean was pretty, bright and buxom, an she
talked a hot blue streak
I would likely just drool on her,
if I ever tried to speak;

She could sing most like an angel,
an her spirit matched her hair,
she was everything I wasn't, she had friends,
and class and flair;

Now that gal was something special,
but I couldn't face the task,
I'd have took her in a minute,
if I hadn't had to ask;

I couldn't show a coward
an I had a little pride,
I just saddled up the Appaloosa stud
an took a ride;

But procrastinatin never gets
a woman off your case,
my sister called me stupid,
mean an rotten to my face;

I was really sweatin bullets,
man she had me in a bind,
never underrate the power
of the partnered female mind,

As time run short sis nagged me,
but I made evasive runs,
so them gals just called my mother
an rolled out the heavy guns;

We had a "come to Jesus" meetin,
an the sermon was by Mom,
the whole valley was expectin
me and Jeanie at the prom;

Jean had bought a full-hooped formal,
petticoats an fancy lace,
and if I stood her up an broke her heart
I'd be a damned disgrace;

I lied poverty an had no car,
but I was throwin flak,

Mom promised me a twenty
an her old black Pontiac;

So finally on the morning of the dance
I did the call,
used the phone for thirty seconds
an asked her to the ball;

Mom somehow scrounged a white corsage,
I showed up at Jean's door,
her folks was both polite, tho they
was burning at the core;

Despite my speech deficiency,
the shindig was a winner,
we danced until they closed it down,
and then we went to dinner;

Then with three other couples,
we joined a shuttle pool,
delivered all the Almo girls
twenty miles from the school;

Them kids took their time a parting,
paused to suck some face a while,
so I didn't have to chatter,
I just took on their style;

After all the doorstep smoochin,
when we got back to my car,
her Dad was there just waitin,
I feared feathers and some tar;

Some years later things got serious,
she didn't take no chance,
she knew I was retarded when it came
to our romance;

Jean arranged my social schedule,
and it wasn't no suggestion,
when she took me out to kiss me up
and then she popped the question;

I thought "this is easy,
getting hitched won't be so bad,"
but I went back to sweatin bullets
when I had to ask her Dad.

THE FLIGHTS OF THE RED NYMPH

Past fifty years you say?
Fifty-three since first I saw
a flash of gold on copper
fling like wind blown halos
floating over avionics, testing
limits of a school yard swing,
freckled nymph of dozen summers
flying heedless over graveled yard,
brashness masking wounds as yet unhealed.
You flew because you could, tethered
above the new, the strange unknown
fleeing cosseted familiar scenes
of orphans, foundlings, mothers surrogate.

Past forty years you say?
Forty-eight, since first we kissed
and you apprised me that I loved you
in a most persuasive way,
lip locked nymph of seventeen
flying headlong through my heartstrings
testing limits of a teenage crush,
brashness masked the longing to belong.
You flew because you willed,
to taste the new, the strange unknown
but tethered still to cosseted familial
scenes of almost daughter by decree.
Past forty-two you say?

Near forty three, since when we pledged
our love, our lives and more
in solemn form, with witnesses,
copper halo misted under white,
modest ring the only dower brought,
flying headstrong into blissful poverty.
We flew because we dreamed,
to share the fruits of love and doubled hope,
into the new, the strange unknown
to cosseted more privy scenes of
sensual and confident belonging.

POST SCRIPT: The lover you are, the verser you get;
for love it ain't free, nor verse neither, yet;
still love's the dance music that warms an old soul;
from a street minuet to the bed rock and roll.

DANCES WITH THE FAT GAL

Gathering light of new born day
air as fine as liquid gold
grass still damp with angels' tears
in God's alfresco dance hall.

Meet alone in hidden place
bough and leaf keep plans our own
sometimes I dance an Arab ballerina
but the Fat Gal comes today.

Electric tension meets my touch
caress, cajole, talk sweet as any lover
offered bribes she responds with disdain
knows I only came for the dance.

Dress quietly in hand-stitched leather
snug up girdle a hitch too tight,
impatience shows by arch of back,
glance of eye, stamp of foot.

Unthankful for silver trim, braided tassel,
bone white binding, she fidgets
waiting for my lead then hops and spins away
spurning attempts to partner up.

Stands me down as she warms to dance
careening about in circles, vertiginous I turn to watch
finally, firm hold on cheek and rein
Fat Gal accepts my lead position.

Dance begins - a few unscripted spins,
sedate and graceful passes around the hall
up and down the hill, across the bridge
some figure eights, circles, side pass or two.

Sun up ends my dance with half-broke mare
Fat Gal dress down,
eat hay, roll on the ground,
same time tomorrow, have a nice day.

WHAT'S IN A NAME?

With pastures tall, but storage brief
we bargained for some mobile beef
some second crop from wagon tiers
we traded for three feeder steers

Our daughter fresh from academe
whose views are strong, if not extreme
playing sophomoric games
blithely asked, "What are their names?"

We just identify our steers
by tag borne numbers on their ears
so we confessed, backs to the wall
they hadn't any names at all

Though names do sometimes cut the
breeze
like "stupid, mangey, and SOBs"
except when in an ugly mood
country folks don't name their food

Disregarding chance of scandals
Meli gave them Christian handles
Cheech and Chong, half angus born
and Beuregard with lengthy horn

Bo aged out of roping school
a husky Corriente fool
Cheech and Chong with Holstein mothers
stood tall and black like feed lot brothers

Bo was never really gracious
thought his name should be Bodacious
and if you let him get too near
he'd forcefully imboss your rear

When the steers were wrapped and frozen
and their favorite cuts were chosen
Cheech and Chong could please the diner
but Bo just somehow tasted finer

Whatever taste buds tell my brain
my mind insists the truth is plain
in spite of what you have been told
revenge is seldom best served cold.

JANUARY

Mercury near zero
Hard packed snow drifts in the wind
chill factor lower,

stream's still open
trick of water passed through a pond,
just iced at the bank

big bales to unload
or horses go hungry, tire chains scratch
hope the tractor starts,

ice cubes on whiskers
ski gloved fingers stiff and numb
its cold as hell today,

ear flaps down, sweater,
insulated coveralls over jeans
you sweat while you freeze,

out here always alive
you shiver, but cozy in the city
you're never sure.

II. FRIENDS & NEIGHBORS

EULALIE AND THE
FIRM FOUNDATION

Though the horsy crowd is tough ones
and they don't seek sympathy
an object of concern became
our neighbor Eulalie;

Limpin into Sunday service
sportin stitches and a sling
a stainless plate with twenty screws
secured a busted wing;

It weren't no scrap with Barry
put her on this painful course
but a frenzied, faunchin, caterwallin
muggin by a horse;

And the culprit wasn't even
Machiavelli on the hoof
just a dunderheaded gelding that
she'd thought was bullet proof;

And she thinks she might have rode him
but he took her unaware
when he blew up unexpected like
and seized her underwear;

He kicked and tipped her forward
lunged and jammed the saddle horn
well up underneath the midriff
of the bra that she had worn;

That bra is space age fabric
tougher than a dollar steak
she could tow a locomotive
and the darn thing wouldn't break;

He pitched and bawled and shaked
and baked and really went to town
so sometimes she was right side up
and sometimes upside down;

She was flailin like a puppet
and it could have come to be
that she got a busted sternum
and a crude mastectomy;

But her left arm took the breakin
slammin on the heavin kack
'til at last the bra let go the horn
and dropped her on her back;

Cuttin horns is made fer grabbin
but when action starts to build
you had better be the grabber
bein' grabbed can git you killed;

Eulalie has done decided
if it wouldn't break no law
when she forks another equine
she ain't gonna wear no bra.

RED ROCK ROUNDUP

Neighbor Tim, pillar of community,
recycled rancher, team roping addict,
rope horse training sponsor of jackpot looptedos,
state police trained, badge carrying
rustler intimidating brand inspector

and reputable churchman all rolled into one
lets scarce hair down on festive occasions
waxing eloquent on good old days
before PETA, OSHA and television
made rodeo less spontaneous;

recalled years back in red rock country
when state college athletic field
served as temporary community rodeo arena
with portable panel chutes and fences
whenever gridiron team was not using it;

sitting horse between steer wrestling runs
Tim watched peripatetic bucking bull
jump makeshift fences, scatter shrieking fans,
and, contesting heavy traffic for right of way,
head for downtown St. George City;

retrieving team roping cordage
Tim and heading/heeling partner
commenced horseback hot pursuit
of fleeing bovine kamikaze fugitive
dodging bug eyed tourists and irate motorists;

finally overtaking winded miscreant
a mile down the busy boulevard
our heroes headed heeled him
stretched him out on the tarmac
waiting for owner to retrieve him;

flustered stock contractor finally caught up
in his heavy hauler Chevy one ton dually
allowed as how he could lead the
critter back to the college, if they
could just tie him to the trailer hitch;

heeler kept rear feet elevated
while header peeled of dallies
dismounted, nervously tied rope
hard and fast to truck's heavy duty
custom made livestock hauling hitch;

heeler shook off heel loop
bull jumped up rested, full of fight
discovering generous slack in rope
lost all interest in following truck
took off again at mach speed;

passing truck on right diagonal
bull hit end of hard twist nylon rope
did involuntary loop the loop front flip
broke his neck and landed dead
flat on his back on courthouse lawn.

THE GREAT HEBER VALLEY RAILROAD HOLDUP – 1970'S STYLE*

Now we all know that crime won't pay
and mischief's even cheaper
but fortune grinned
when cowboys sinned
and the Wild Bunch from Weber High
held up the Heber Creeper;

Tho' high school finals rodeo
had promised fame and honor
with first runs scored
the kids got bored
the slack between their roping
rounds became a real yawner;

Then they discovered armaments
at local toy providers
each got a gun
and had some fun
shooting cocky rough stock guys
and pretty barrel riders;

The Heber Valley railroad
fired up its antique train
the boiler steamed
the whistle screamed
it huffed and puffed t'ward Deer Creek
crossing mostly flat terrain;

The Wild Bunch soon hatched a plan
to stage some real West action
each forked a steed
and left at speed
to catch the train and shoot some folks
and savor their reaction;

They shot through open windows as
they passed each ancient car
their victims cheered
and clapped or jeered
as brakes engaged the squealing Creeper
stopped with doors ajar;

With their water pistols empty
and their courage winding down
reaction unexpected
further plan neglected
the Wild Bunch turned tail
and retreated back to town;

Like a ranch dog crouching
waiting for a passing car to harry
with one track mind
no goal defined
the Wild Bunch had not a clue
when they finally caught their quarry.

III. HAYSEED HAIKU

A FEW HAIKU IN
LATE FEBRUARY

Snow deep and drifted
brace of honkers flying low
portend early thaw

Sun warms south porches
orange and black spots on wall
Box Elder bugs move

Mud envelops gravel
frost dissolving transforms lane
into foot deep ruts

Flash white on orange
hunting cold bunkered gophers
a fox reappears

Fast moving storm passed
leaving a rolling fog bank
foothills invisible

By mothers' tongues
calves born on frigid nights
will mostly survive

Flattened and frozen
his essence still lingers
dead skunk on blacktop

Waiting for green grass
mares bellies distended
too early to foal

MARCH HAIKU

Under moldy hay
lurk unpleasant surprises
goats heads await sun

Droplets roll slowly
down from snow drift cornices
refreezing at dusk

Energetic voles
scurry about the surface
cats catch and eat them

Starting as cool breeze
and growing to blizzard force
Winter still with us

APRIL HAIKU

Young snow on the ground
horse tails turned to the wind
happy all fools day

Fresh from a green house
in front of historic homes
tulip bulbs flower

Dormant pasture grass
awaits warm breeze and sun
dry hay still feeds cows

Mountain slopes display
bare shoulders as snow retreats
prepare for blossoms

Automobiles show
best sign of changing season
bugs splatter windshield

Simple forms survive
and emerge when seasons change
worms seldom frozen

MAY HAIKU

Fresh new garden tossed
like baby veggie salad
wind and hail passed by

Pastures and hillsides
preternaturally green
before sun dries to brown

Grass moves in sensual
undulating terrestrial waves
horses shine like copper

Burrowing rodent
survives flood and plow
gopher not mortal

Budding wild flowers
begin to show bright orange
color hides new sand burrs

WINTER HAIKU

Snow falls on dry leaves
Birds compete for rare morsels
Robins are still here

Old drifts survive thaw
Small creatures walk over crusts
Fox speeds across ice

Cold stiffens live things
Life slows down in frigid air
Old mare can't get up

AUGUST HAIKU

False dawn wakes blackbirds,
dew condenses on mown hay
Red Tail strikes breakfast

Blazing sun returns,
clouds flee on desiccated air
log walls harbor cool

Grass transmutes to brown
alfalfa roots reach deeper
still touching moisture

Fattening cattle
lounge under hawthorn bowers
horses disdain shade

Brace of doves alight,
scratching up dropped feed grain
fledglings flown away

Black stink bugs abound,
hornet's paper nests increase
grasshoppers rule field

Storm front crossed valley,
micro-bursts break old wheel lines
no measured rain

No time for riding
summer toil diverts riders
horses vacation

Masked marauders
strip corn husks for evening meals
don't touch tomatoes

Night follows sundown,
cool breeze flows down North Canyon
lone coyote sings

Farm dogs voice reprise
of wild cousin's yodeling
cats yowl counterpoint

IV. REVISIONIST HISTORY

THE SNOW HORSE

Many snows before the White Eyes brought the plow and iron horse,
the spirits in their seasons taught the People wisdom's course;

The Utah and Shoshone shared this desert valley home,
with the spirits and their handiwork, their teachers and their tome;

Knew they well the way of Winter, when the Cold Man's lance and steed,
drove the wounded Summer, Sun Man, to the South to rest and bleed;

From the Moon of Falling Leaves until the Moon of Birth and Flower,
Cold Man ruled the valley, from his blizzard shrouded bower;

But the Sun Man was resurgent as he healed and gathered strength,
in the Moon of Greening Grasses he'd begin to win at length;

But the people knew the Cold Man hadn't given up the fight,
til he tied his horse up on the ridge and made his northward flight;

When the Snow Horse showed up on the ridge Sun Man was in control,
no Cold Man charging through the clouds to vex the Peoples' soul;

The bounding Forkhorn fattened and the hunters took new heart,
the Sego bulbs were swelling and the diggers did their part;

As the Snow Horse slowly melted, fear of hunger melted too,
roasted crickets made fine flower, birds and rabbits made fine stew;

Holy men divined the spirits, but they couldn't understand,
how or why the tribes of White Eyes warred to dominate their land;

First the White Eyes wanted beaver, just passed on if left alone,
then a few began to linger building forts of sticks and stone;

So the Snow Horse took new meaning, when the Sun Man cleared the trails,
the White Eyes tribe called Mormons came with wagons, plows and rails;

The valley was the People's, but when Sun Man warmed the snows,
the Mormons plowed it up to make it "blossom as a rose";

The White Eyes killed the game and then diverted all the streams,
the People fell to illness, pain, despair and whiskey dreams;

When their game grew scarce the People asked the spirits what to eat,
the Sun Man sent them crickets in the Moon of Dust and Heat;

But the Mormons' patron spirits, as their grain came into head,
brought down gulls in countless numbers to devour the Peoples' bread;

The spirits and the holy men then lost the People's trust,
like the Snow Horse, they just melted, and scattered in the dust;

But the seasons keep revolving, Snow Horse Ridge is up there still,
White Eye farmers scan the Snow Horse for the time to plant and till.

THE BALLAD OF OLD EPHRAIM

When campfires have burned past their glory
and scout masters tales become gory,
as the embers burn low
by the last ruddy glow
they always recite "the bear story;"

The story is now near a hundred years old
but it still sends a chill every time it is told
how he came in the dark
and the dogs' futile bark
might be ended by death – quick and cold,

Old Ephraim the grizzly weighed over a ton
the sheepherders hated the wily old son,
he gobbled their mutton
like a demonic glutton
while slyly evading both steel trap and gun,

But finally one night in a high Wasatch draw
Old Ephraim was caught in a trap by one paw,
in deep beaver dam mud,
as steel jaws drew his blood
he roared hate and pain from his foam slavered maw,

The trap was chained off to a huge fallen log
which lay at the edge of the beaver made bog,
but with great ursine strength
he dislodged it at length
and tugged it away in a three-legged slog,

The trap-setting shepherd roused out of his camp
with his carbine in hand through the dark and the damp
as the bear rumbled near
he was pumping with fear
and occasional lightning was his only lamp,

He fired his gun as Old Ephraim came on
and kept shooting until his last cartridge was gone,
though at last the bear fell
it was too dark to tell
that Old Ephraim had expired, until dawn,

They buried his bones in the draw where he died,
the sheepherder probably salvaged his hide,
he was the biggest and last,
the Utah grizzly is past,
but his skull is still the Smithsonian's pride

V. THEOLOGY

AMAZING GRACE - HALL'S VERSES:

Amazing grace, how kind the plan
That buys a bond-child free
I'd still be bound, but Son of Man
Thou paid the price for me[1]

Resplendent day, I'm Adam's child
Cold death my destiny
But Jesus Christ, redeemer mild
We all shall rise with thee

Most fervent hope, my heart beats filled
With what I poorly see
Christ's passion-blood, in droplets spilled
Thou passed through hell for me

Transcendent word, most welcome sound
That says I'm loved of thee
I'm lost in doubts, but still I'm found
Thine arms encircle me

Atoning gift, I can't repay
My savior's bounteous love
My offered mite, I seek thy way
It's marked full paid above

Renewing peace, thou asked not more
Than my poor self can give
My heart, a willing mind, my chore,
to follow thee and live

---

1 Traditional Protestant Gospel Hymn Lyrics by John Newton:
    Amazing grace, how sweet the sound
    That saved a wretch like me
    I once was lost, but now I'm found
    Was blind, but now I see

END GAME

At fourscore ten the end game plays
too soon, too late, unwelcome and relentless,
acrid, bitter taste, as milk gone sour, curdled and offensive
visibly degrading, slipping part from part
element from element, sustenance to detrius,
a sorcerer's perverse formula steadily turning gold to lead.

Darkness seeps from corners
drowning sight and motion
quiet mourning grief for losses beyond feeling
familiar comforts of love, a face, a touch
are stolen, lost in dim memory.

Solitary in the stream of life
a ghost ship shrouded in the mists
as laden vessels pass unhailed, unheeding
pain, the only friend who understands,
bids touch of death, her only certain succor
so slip half willing into sweet and warm eternity.

WHY GOD MUST BE A HORSEMAN

One time in the chill of the season
as the long winter night made its fall,
we set by the fire in the bunkhouse
and debated the way of it all

Of whether there's horses in heaven,
an if any such heavenly steeds
have got white feathered wings like them
angels, an halos to harold their deeds

Ben reckoned that feathers on horses
was mostly a myth of the Greeks,
an likely would just be a nuisance
when rode through the brush an the creeks

If there's heavenly cattle to gather
an heavenly leppies to rope,
Lew reckoned them angel-type
waddies would be fouled up an losing all hope

If a heavenly horseman was fixin to
give his old noose a wide swing,
it would rickochet off of a halo
if it didn't hang up on a wing

I was put out to hear such malarkey,
pure sacrilege raises my hair,
I donno about feathers or halos,
but I'm sure they got horses up there

I hear tell about the Almighty,
that he's got unconditional love,
I donno how he could have learned it,
without having horses above

Now some dogs as have made my acquaintance
have been faithful and true to the end,
but I never have yet met a canine
that would work plumb to death for a friend

An I hear as how patience with mankind
is sort of a heavenly trait,
I 'pect He learned that from good horses,
that had worked on this side of his gate

So that's how I know He's a horseman,
He's got virtues shared most with the horse,
He's teachin them virtues to mankind,
an his messenger's equine of course.

NIGHTMARES OF ST. JOHN THE DIVINE (REVELATIONS 6)

I woke from a dream one dark morning
all shaky and covered with sweat
my mind in a frenzied condition
holding scenes that I'd rather forget

I thought that I looked at the future
viewing as best I could tell
four grim apocalypse horses
delivering portents of Hell

I imagined a glimpse of Bin Laden
grasping a bow and a crown
on the stolen white steed of Mohammed
bringing the Twin Towers down

A gore covered red horse responded
with legions of swordsmen astride
shedding blood through the lands of the prophet
where his most zealous eagerly died

Another horse stalked out of Wall Street
in a coat that was blackened with crude
bearing scales that move all of our commerce
in the hands of the ruthless and shrewd

While a loud voice recited the prices
"Buy oil at one fifty today"
"Four coins for a gallon of diesel"
"Two hundred for one ton of hay"

"Twenty coins for a measure of barley"
borrow to pay if you will
but the lenders are all on the black horse
and nothing is left in their till

Vaguely I saw that a grullo was
leading all third world parades
the rider delivering misery
with genocide, bird flu and AIDS

I wakened my lovely companion
to warn her that Hell claimed it's due
and I quickly recounted my nightmare
wondering what we should do

She gently said we should be sleeping
that nothing I told her brought tears
we had heard it all in the headlines
over the past seven years

You're really not much of psychic
she said in a bit of a huff
come back to bed you big sissy
we've already survived all that stuff.

BELLS OF YULETIDE

Gather children of all ages
hear the carols, smell the smells
feel the wonder that is Christmas,
to the singing of the bells
to the shouting and the soaring syncopation
of the bells.

Hear the ancient natal story
as the Christ child's story swells
in your heart the gift of giving
move in concert with the bells
with crying and the chiming
and the calling of the bells.

VI. WESTERN WHIMSY

THE GOOD LIFE

The other day in Salty Town amid the
noise and heat,
I chanced to meet a rancher friend a
limpin down the street;

We howdied, an he asked about my health
an hardihood,
I told him that my pains was few
an I was eatin good;

I mentioned how I'd had the gout, an my
kidneys sometimes stone me,
how I put two horses down last year,
But not them as had thrown me;

He sez, son, count your blessins, an
stay with your life of crime,
you're drawing cash now regular,
don't never ranch full time;

He sez while ridin fence last month
he smelt a awful stench,
some yahoo killed
his white face bull out on a brushy bench;

His wife an cook has fallen ill, cashed her
last chocolate chip,
An the Doc is just about to slice
a tumor off his lip;

His hired man don't work half-time, he's
always in his cups,
His little heeler bitch just had twelve
worthless weiner pups;

His well's gone dry, his baler's stuck,
his broke leg ain't quite healed,
his mowed and rained-on hay
is moldin nicely in the field;

From ring bone, founder, twisted gut,
his cavy's mighty lean,
one little cayuse mule to ride,
"Slick Willie's" tough and mean;

His pickup truck is wind broke too, its swallowed
too much dust,
His tractor has the trembles, cause
the tank is full of rust;

They've cut his BLM permits, the bank
just called his loans,
five hours a night don't hardly soothe
the achin in his bones;

I ventured how he'd be advised
to dump that sorry place,
He could retire, an just live out his years
with joy and grace;

He reckoned that would come
in pairs, with rodeos in China,
cause Joy has septicemia
an Grace has bad angina;

He sez nobody understands the joys
of life with cattle,
an the healthy smell of week old sweat
that complements the battle;

Besides he couldn't bear to
lose that pile of dust an stone,
it's a permanent concession, for him
to bitch and moan.

A LITTLE CHAMBER MUSIC

My wife come home from town last week,
told me don't fly the coop,
sez we was headin back to hear
some chamber music group.

She sez a civic minded crowd had
gave the town some soul,
an arts and humans council had
put culture on a roll.

She said important folks was there
an' we should look our best,
I scraped the barnyard off my boots
an' dusted off my vest.

I donno why she cared at all
town folks is no great shakes,
their phony smiles is all store bought
and their kids is all mistakes.

When them musicians took their seats
I thought someone would sing,
but they played some oriental bit
they said was called "too ning."

It grated on my tortured ears
but I never guessed the score,
As that's the best they had to give
in their lengthy repertour.

I've rousted caterwallin' cats
an' heard a buzzard cry,
I've heard the scream a stuck pig makes
when he's about to die.

I've sat down in an ambulance
among the crushed and maimed,
an' listened to the moans an' cries
an' never been so shamed.

I've ran my nails down the slate
an' heard the blackboard shriek,
I know the sound my mama made
while fallin' the creek.

But I ain't never in my life
endured such painful stings,
like dental drills' vibrations
from them chamber music strings.

My face got pale as bread dough
an' my shirt was soaked with sweat,
I was prayin' for relief,
but they warn't near done yet.

When they called an intermission
I could barely crawl around,
an' a buzzin' on my eardrums
shorly warn't the Nashville sound.

I don't believe they understood
them tears upon my cheek,
them town folks was ecstatic
but I was feelin' mighty weak.

Them musicians reassembled
An' I trembled when I sat,
But they never missed a measure
when I upchucked in my hat.

My wife was durned embarrassed
and her patience was wore thin,
So she dragged to the pickup truck
an' sorta poured me in.

Though I'm feelin' good as ever
an' my belly's settled down,
an' tonight's another concert
she won't let me go to town.

So I'm sitting cogitatin
Funk 'n Wagnall's on the bar,
How they must have named that music
From "chamber, torture" and "Chamber, Star."

GOOSED

A migratory gaggle in the customary wedge
circled low to make a pit stop where the tulles met the sedge

As the vee flight crossed the skyline I did a double take
counting seven hefty honkers and a little Mallard drake

Somewhere in the southland someone paid the extra fare
to upgrade the drake from the Quacker Fly to Canada Goose Air

The numbers posed a puzzle and my consternation grew
goose counts in spring migration are divisible by two

The Branta Canadensis know that they must mate for life
and the unit for migration is the gander and his wife

So the case seems quite compelling though his moral code is loose
that this little rascal Mallard drake had hooked up with a goose

The prospects for this union seem on shaky ground at best
since Mallard drakes have wandering eyes and don't stay in the nest

It's uncertain if size matters to a starry eyed goose bride
but a clash of cultures seldom lets domestic bliss abide

As Mallard hens know, Mallard drakes are summer loves at most
when fall arrives the drake moves on, their union now is toast

I'm guessing fall migration finds a single goose in flight
with no goslings and no mate to share the annual southward rite.

HALF BROTHERS

If the foliage on your physog
forms a foot long double "u"
and your hide and chinks are weathered
to a rather reddish hue,

If you ride the rugged ridges
with a rocky basin crew
and there's shiny silver somethings
on their tack and spade bits too,

If you dally a riata
to a slick fork Wade thumb screw
and you tie a yard of fabric
on your neck to turn the dew,

If you favor flat fedoras
and a packer is your shoe
I salute you little brother
you're a ruddy buckaroo

If the Marlboro man's your model
for the macho style review
and you favor shotgun leggings
with a Texas star tattoo,

If you bust the brushy bastions
where the bovines hide and moo
or pursue them on the prairie
where the short grass always grew,

If a grazer bar's the only bit
your horse will ever chew
and your saddle's set full double
with a rope you can't undo,

If your hat's a hard shell taco
and a low cut boot will do
power to you 'nother brother
flatland cowboy through and through.

THE SHAMING OF THE SHREW

Ols Olson's cheap he handles sheep
and drives a grey Toyota
in mutton sales his family hails
from rural North Dakota

Carlotta squeals and wears spike heels
her name was Pacifíco
she's not to blame her family came
from sunny Puerto Rico

Carlotta yearns for wit that burns
and lively conversation
for feelings bared and passions dared
and constant stimulation

But Ole heeds the style of Swedes
where gut spill spells disgrace
he hems and haws and clamps his jaws
and wears a poker face

When Ole said, "I thee do wed"
to fiery dark Carlotta,
he set his heart to play the part
and treat her like he oughta

Carlotta vowed she'd not be cowed
her intrigue ran blood-red
she'd rant and cuss and start a fuss
to wake the living dead

She thought it right to pick a fight
with strategy demonic
she yelled and swore and stamped the floor
while Ole waxed laconic

Her voice grew tired though she was wired
while he was breaking bread
she did apply a shepherd's pie
on top of Ole's head

He never spoke nor missed a stroke
'til he had finished supper
he spooned his hair 'til it was bare
then tagged the meal a fixer-upper

Hot spuds feel great upon my pate
and make my hair all wavy
but truth to tell my latin belle
it needs a touch more gravy.

VII. MISCELLANEOUS RANTS

BELLS FOR THE DAMNED

Gather vagabond and royal with the pestilential smells
of their deeds of desecration to the crying of the bells,
to the clanging and the clanking and
the clamor of the bells,

From the gallows and the statehouse through the caverns and the dells
lead the ego bloated butchers through the pounding of the bells,
through the popping and the pinging and
the pealing of the bells.

Marching dark in gore and bleakness morbid legions from the cells
take their path to sure perdition and reverberating bells,
and the roaring and the rattle and
the raging of the bells,

All the raped and murdered children lie like tattered bagatelles
in mute witness of the justice in the tumult of the bells,
in the thudding and the throbbing and
the thunder of the bells,

Here the incandescent vapors of a hundred thousand hells
light the way to the inferno through the babble of the bells,
through the bonging and the banging and
the braying of the bells,

And the stern expostulation of a voiceless million swells
in one voice of condemnation with the shouting of the bells,
with the slamming and the smashing and
the shrieking of the bells,

Standing surrogates for victims score cacaphonistic knells
as a thousand hard rock demons mind the tolling of the bells,
mind the tumult and the
tintinnabulations of the bells.

NON ILLIGITIMI CARBORUNDUM

tectonic plates grinding
monotonic millstone turning
gin tonic prattle wearing away
alluvion, grist, pinstriped pinheads
creating, exhaling, gathering dust

Sisyphus' burden rolled by gravity not by the gods
free market free-fall fueled by primal fear
religious/political right are not
religious/political left not right either

reducio ad absurdum:

to the victor go the spoiled,
the early worm gets the bird,
eat drink and be merry -
tomorrow file bankruptcy,
cast your bread upon waters -
it does not return through oil troubled waters,
race is not to the swift nor battle to the strong-
until after a drug test,
loose lips sink kooks.